C000264702

Printed in Great Britain
by Amazon

24746030R00070